GW01066264

My Life, My Words

Remembering Mahatma Gandhi

"You must be the change
you wish to see in the world."

My Life, My Words

Remembering Mahatma Gandhi

Text Editor: Sangeeta Kochhar

Flag Foundation
of India, New Delhi

Etch: An imprint of
Natraj Publishers

The book has been published in collaboration with the Flag Foundation of India. It is a non-profit registered society that aims to promote unity through the positive embodiment and celebration of the National Flag. It is inspired by and based on Mahatma Gandhi's principles of brotherhood and non-violence.

Flag Foundation of India, 171, South Avenue, New Delhi 110011
Tel: +91- 11-23012253, 23795299 Fax: +91-11-23012213
Email:info@flagfoundationofindia.in   Website: www.flagfoundationofindia.in

The Publishers and the Flag Foundation of India wish to thank Ms. Tara Gandhi and Dr. Savita Singh of Gandhi Smriti for their gracious support and co-operation. The photographs in the book have been reproduced from the archives at Gandhi Smriti with their kind permission.

The cartoons have been reproduced with the permission of www.gandhiserve.org.

First Published 2011
© Etch: An imprint of Natraj Publishers
ISBN: 978-81-8158-109-9

Book Design: Arati Devasher, www.aratidevasher.com

Published by Upendra Arora for Etch, an imprint of Natraj Publishers.
Printed in India.

Contents

Message from the Flag Foundation

The 60th death anniversary of Mahatma Gandhi is a solemn moment, a time when all the citizens of India would be well advised to revisit the Mahatma's profoundly important philosophies and beliefs. In an India, where religion, caste, region and language still play an all important and often divisive role even sixty years after independence there is s strong need to reorient ourselves towards our common 'Indian' identity. The Flag Foundation was set up with this—a unity around the tricolour—as one of its main objectives. And we strongly believe in Gandhi ji's views on a secular and democratic country where non-violence takes primacy over all else. Sadly, this isn't the way India has turned out, and Bapu would be unhappy over the state of affairs in many parts of India today.

Albert Einstein said about him, "I believe Gandhi's views were the most enlightened of all the political men in our time. We should strive to do things in his spirit: not to use violence in fighting for our cause, but by nonparticipation in anything you believe is evil."

This book is an attempt to reintroduce Mahatma Gandhi to the mainstream. It is designed and structured in a way to appeal to all ages and groups of people. The youth are the future of our country and very few have had a proper introduction to Gandhi's most important teachings, values and beliefs. This book, by collecting his finest pearls of wisdom offers readers a simple yet profound introduction to Gandhi's life and words.

We believe that the world would be a better place if people followed the path of Gandhi or at least inculcated some of his values. With this book Flag Foundation of India sets out to claim those souls who are willing to die for their country's cause, but for no cause willing to kill. Humanity owes the twenty first century no better gift than this.

FLAG FOUNDATION of INDIA

—Shallu Jindal
Vice President, Flag Foundation of India

Foreword

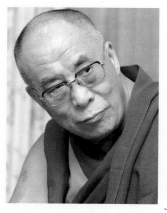

Mahatma Gandhi has been a source of inspiration to me ever since I was a small boy growing up in Tibet. He was a great human being with a deep understanding of human nature. He made every effort to encourage the full development of the positive aspects of the human potential and to reduce or restrain the negative. Therefore, I find it most encouraging to know that his life, in his deeds and words, continues to be a source of inspiration today in our rapidly changing world.

Personally, I have been deeply inspired by Mahatma Gandhi's adoption of ahimsa or non-violence in India's freedom struggle. I have, therefore, put this into practice in my own efforts to restore the fundamental human rights and freedoms of the Tibetan people. I also admire the simplicity of Gandhiji's way of life. Although he was well versed in modern, western knowledge, he remained an Indian and lived a simple life in accordance with ancient Indian philosophy. What is more, Gandhiji was aware of the problems of the common people.

I am grateful for this opportunity to pay tribute to Mahatma Gandhi because I consider myself to be his follower. On the one hand, I consider the cultivation of non-violence and compassion as part of my own daily practice, not because it is something holy or sacred, but because it is of practical benefit to me. Trying to cultivate non-violence and compassion gives me satisfaction; it gives me a peace that provides a ground for maintaining sincere, genuine relationships with other people. One of the most important things we all have to realise is that human happiness is interdependent. Our own successful or happy future is very much related to that of others. Therefore, helping others or having consideration for their rights and needs is actually not just a matter of responsibility, but involves our own happiness.

Another important aspect of the Mahatma's legacy is his insistence on the importance of truth. His practice of non-violence depended wholly on the power of truth. This collection of Gandhiji's words and the various images that accompany them allows us to remind ourselves of the truth he espoused and expressed.

——The Dalai Lama
Dharamsala, India

Introduction

'Words are few, when the heart is full'.... Any attempt to have a look at the wonderful personality of a man, who has been so human and yet does not belong to the world of us mortals, makes one feel that one has taken an inner flight to reach him. Friends who brought out *My Life, My Words* need to be congratulated for giving one a moment of bliss, which is worth cherishing.

I recall my first darshan of Mahatma Gandhi when I was a little girl. We lived in Nagpur, my hometown, close to Gandhiji's Sevagram Ashram. That day I was sent by my mother along with my brother to receive my uncle who was coming by the Bombay Howrah Mail. When we reached the railway station, we found a huge crowd. People were shouting "Mahatma Gandhi ki Jai". I learnt that Gandhiji was travelling by the same train. I joined the crowd. Someone shouted, this little girl will be crushed, protect her. They all pushed me towards Gandhiji's compartment. Gandhiji was standing at the door of his third class compartment, waving to the people and I was standing just at the feet of the Mahatma. The sounds of 'Jai-Jai' were rising every moment. The train stops at Nagpur for half an hour. I was so spellbound that all the while I just kept looking at Bapu, forgetting completely that I had a job to fulfil. Bapu's magnetic personality had a deep impact on my mind. After the train moved and the people dispersed, I came out from a trance...May be that was the moment when I decided to devote my life to the mission of the Mahatma.

Mahatma Gandhi's life and words are like the Parasmani that can transform even ugly iron into glittering gold. Let this reach those who are in the evening of their lives, so that they can have peace, and let this reach those who are still experiencing the dawn of life, so that they will ever live in that beautiful state of life. Let this reach those whose learning is taking them to cynicism, so that they know what true learning is. Let it reach those who belong to the category of the great Kabir, and those who have never touched a pen and paper, so that they can all strive to write divine poetry. The

immortal Mahatma lives in his words, and he also lives beyond all words. It is a truth, that he lives for ever, and no bullets have the capacity to harm his eternal life.

To present all aspects of Gandhiji's life and words is a near impossibility. But what is needed to give a touch of immortality is not an ocean of nectar. Just a drop of nectar can do that miracle. That is exactly the objective of this book. The countless readers who would get an opportunity to glance through the book are sure to express their satisfaction.

All good wishes from someone, for whom Gandhi lives. Forever.

—Nirmala Deshpande
Member of Parliament

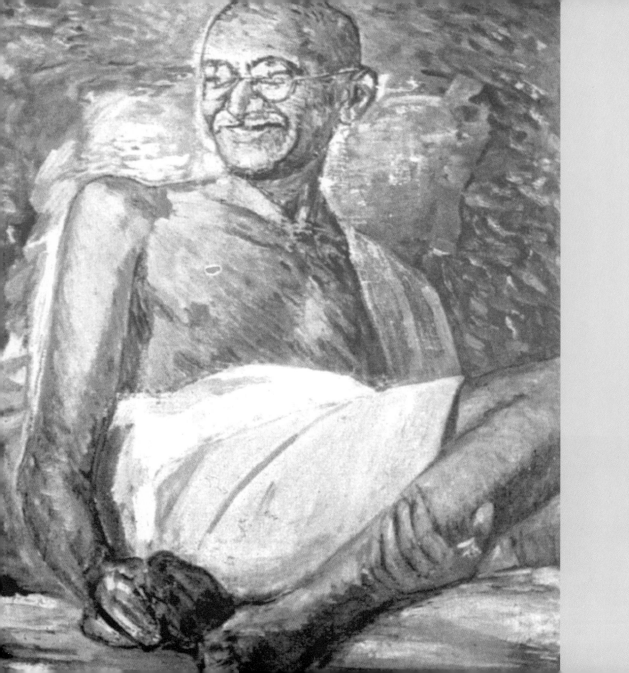

On Truth

"Mine may today be a voice in the wilderness, but it will be heard when all other voices are silenced, if it is the voice of truth."

"The highest truth needs no communicating, for it is by its very nature self propelling. It radiates its influence silently as the rose its fragrance without the intervention of a medium."

�֍

"To a true artist only that face is beautiful which, quite apart from its exterior, shines with the truth within the soul."

✖

"I believe that honesty is the best policy, surely whilst I so believe, I must be honest in thought, word and deed; otherwise I become an impostor."

✖

"A cause can only lose by exaggeration."

✖

"It is more correct to say that truth is God than to say that God is truth."

"Devotion to truth is the sole justification for our existence. All our activities should be centered in truth. Truth should be the very breath of our life. Once this stage in the pilgrim's progress is reached, all other rules of correct living will come without effort, and obedience to them will be instinctive. But without truth it is impossible to observe any principles or rules in life."

✕

"I believe in what Max Mueller said years ago, namely that truth needed to be repeated as long as there were men who disbelieved it."

✕

"Truth … is what the voice within tells you. …
What may be truth for one may be untruth for another."

✕

"I found the nearest approach to truth is through love. But I found also that love has many meanings… it is very difficult to understand that God is love because of the variety of meanings of love, but I never found a double meaning in connection with truth…."

"My uniform experience has convinced me that there is no other God than Truth. … The only means for the realisation of Truth is ahimsa. … However sincere my strivings after ahimsa may have been, they have still been imperfect and inadequate. The little fleeting glimpses, therefore, that I have been able to have of Truth can hardly convey an idea of the indescribable lustre of Truth, a million times more intense than that of the sun we daily see in our eyes. In fact what I have caught is only the faintest glimmer of that mighty effulgence…. I can say with assurance, as a result of all my experiments, that a perfect vision of Truth can only follow a complete realisation of ahimsa. To see the universal and all-pervading Spirit of Truth face to face one must be able to love the meanest of creation as oneself."

"The way of peace is the way of truth.
Truthfulness is even more important than peacefulness."

"I know that man who forsakes truth can forsake
his country and his nearest and dearest ones."

✗

"There is no truth in a man who cannot control his tongue."

✗

"I have learnt a lot during these days of quiet thinking. What have you?
Could you assure me that you will never repeat your mistake? You may
err again but this fast will be lost on you if you do not realise the way out
of it. Truthfulness is the master key. Do not lie under any circumstances
whatsoever. Keep nothing secret, take your teachers and your elders into
your confidence and make a clean breast of everything to them. Bear ill
will to none, do not say an evil thing of anyone behind his back, above all
"to thine own self be true", so that you are false to no one else. Truthful
dealing even in the least little thing of life is the only secret of a pure life."

"Almost every day brings the announcement of another book about Gandhi. In one way that is inevitable. Men will not be able to take their eyes off him. It is also profoundly encouraging and makes every book about Gandhi an event in the history of the atomic age."

—A.J.Munste
in Muriel Lester's *Gandhi's Signature*

On Faith and God

"There are times when you have to obey a call which is the highest of all, i.e. the voice of conscience, even though such obedience may cost many a bitter tear, and even more; separation from friends, from family, from the state to which you may belong and from all that you have held as dear as life itself. For his obedience is the law of our being."

"Everyone who wills can hear the inner voice, it is within everyone."

✄

"Exercise of faith will be the safest where there is a clear determination summarily to reject all that is contrary to truth and love."

✄

"But for my faith in God, I should have been a raving maniac."

✄

"In his boundless love God permits the atheism of the atheist."

✄

"When I admire the wonders of a sunset or the beauty of the moon, my soul expands in the worship of the creator. If we could all give our own definitions of God, there would be as many definitions as there are men and women."

"God's word is 'He who strives never perishes'.
I have implicit faith in that promise."

"He who would be friends with God must remain alone,
or make the whole world his friend."

"God seems to be as cruel as he is merciful."

"God is that indefinable something which we all feel but which we do not know. To me God is Truth and Love. God is ethics and morality. God is fearlessness, God is the source of light and life and yet He is above and beyond all these. God is conscience. He transcends speech and reason. He is a personal God to those who need His touch. He is the purest essence. He simply Is to those who have faith. He is long suffering. He is patient but He is also terrible. He is the greatest democrat the world knows. He is the greatest tyrant ever known. We are not. He Is."

"Mankind is notoriously too dense to read the signs that God sends from time to time. We require drums to be beaten into our ears before we should wake from our trance and hear the warning and see that to lose oneself in all is the only way to find oneself."

�֍

"God is a very hard taskmaster. He is never satisfied with fireworks display. His mills although they grind surely and incessantly grind excruciatingly slow and he is never satisfied with hasty forfeitures of life. It is a sacrifice of the purest that he demands, and so you and I have prayerfully to plod on, live out the life so long as it is vouchsafed to us to live it."

✖

"I need no inspiration other than Nature's. She has never failed me yet. She mystifies me, bewilders me, sends me into ecstasies. Besides God's handiwork, does not man's fade into insignificance?"

✖

"Before the throne of the Almighty man will be judged not by his acts but by his intentions. For God alone reads our hearts."

"I do dimly perceive that whilst everything around me is ever changing, ever dying, there is underlying all that change a living power that is changeless, that holds all together, that creates, dissolves and recreates. That informing power or spirit is God. And since nothing else I see merely through the senses can or will persist, He alone is. And is this power benevolent or malevolent? I see it as purely benevolent, for I can see that in the midst of death life persists, in the midst of untruth truth persists, in the middle of darkness light persists. Hence I gather that God is Life, Truth, Light. He is Love. He is the supreme Good."

"There is orderliness in the universe; there is an unalterable law governing everything and every being that exists or lives. It is not a blind law; for no blind law can govern the conduct of living beings....The Law which governs all life is God. Law and the Lawgiver are one. I may not deny the Law or the Law-Giver because I know so little about It or Him."

"My faith is brightest in the midst of impenetrable darkness."

"Even though Gandhi practised his religion with courage and consistency, he had an unusual sense of humour, a certain lightheartedness, even gaiety, which we do not associate with ardent religious souls. This playfulness was the outcome of an innocence of heart, a spontaneity of spirit."

—Sarvapalli Radhakrishnan

INDIAN ROPE TRICK

On Religion and Atheism

"Religions are not for separating men from one another, they are meant to bind them. It is a misfortune that today they are so distorted that they have become a potent cause of strife and mutual slaughter."

"One's own religion is after all a matter between oneself and one's Maker and no one else."

"Every formula of every religion has in this age of reason, to submit to the acid test of reason and universal assent."

"A religious act cannot be performed with aid of the bayonet or the bomb."

"That religion and that nation will be blotted out of the face of earth which pins its faith to injustice, untruth or violence."

"Of all the animal creations of God, man is the only animal who has been created in order that he may know his maker. Man's aim in life is not therefore to add from day to day to his material prospects and to his material possessions, but his predominant calling is, from day to day to come nearer to his own Maker."

✖

"As soon as we lose the moral basis, we cease to be religious."

✖

" If we are imperfect ourselves, religion as conceived by us must also be imperfect. We have not realised religion in its perfection, even as we have not realised God. Religion of our conception, being thus imperfect, is always subject to a process of evolution and reinterpretation. Progress towards Truth, towards God, is possible only because of such an evolution."

"I cannot conceive politics as divorced from religion.
Indeed religion should pervade every one of our actions. Here
religion does not mean sectarianism. It means a belief in ordered
moral government of the universe.... This religion transcends
Hinduism, Islam, Christianity, etc. It does not supersede them. It
harmonises them and gives them reality."

✕

"The study of other religions besides one's own will give a grasp of the
rock-bottom unity of all religions and afford a glimpse also of the universal
and absolute truth which lies beyond the 'dust of creeds and faiths.' Let no
one even for a moment entertain the fear that a reverent study of other
religions is likely to weaken or shake one's faith in one's own."

"It is a tragedy that religion for us means, today nothing more than restrictions on food and drink, nothing more than adherence to absence of superiority and inferiority."

✗

"There are some who in the egotism of their reason declare that they have nothing to do with religion. But it is like a man saying that he breathes but that he has no nose. Whether by reason, or by instinct, or by superstition, man acknowledges some sort of relationship with the Divine. The rankest agnostic or atheist does not acknowledge the need of moral principle, and associates something good with its observance and something bad with its non-observance.... Even a man who disowns religion cannot, and does not, live without religion."

A charming letter Gandhi wrote to the children at the Ashram when he was in Yervada Jail:

Little Birds,

Ordinary birds cannot fly without wings. With wings, of course, all can fly. But if you, without wings, will learn how to fly, then all your troubles will indeed be at an end. And I will teach you.

See, I have no wings, yet I come flying to you everyday in thought. Look, here is little Vimala, here is Hari, and here is Dharmakumar. And you also can come flying to me in thought.

There is no need for a teacher for those who know how to think. The teacher may guide us; but he cannot give us the power of thinking. That is latent in us. Those who are wise get wise thoughts.

Tell me who, amongst you, are not praying properly in Pranubhai's evening prayer.

Send me a letter signed by all and those who do not know how to sign may make a cross.

Bapu's Blessings

On Prayer

"Prayer is not asking, it is longing of the soul. It is daily admission of one's weakness. It is better in prayer to have a heart without words than words without a heart."

"There is an eternal struggle raging in man's breast between the powers of darkness and of light, and he, who has not the sheet-anchor of prayer to rely upon, will be a victim to the powers of darkness."

✗

"When a man wants to make up with his maker, he does not consult a third party."

✗

"Each one prays to God according to his own light."

✗

"Virtue lies in being absorbed in one's prayers in the presence of din and noise."

"For those who are filled with the presence of God in them, to labour is to pray. Their life is one continuous prayer, or act of worship."

✗

"Prayer needs no speech. It is in itself independent of any sensuous effort. I have not the slightest doubt that prayer is an unfailing means of cleansing the heart of passions. But it must be combined with utmost humility."

✗

"I feel life more in tune with the infinite when I am silent, though I agree that we should always be in tune with it, whether we are silent or speaking, whether we are in solitude or in a bustling crowd."

"Idolatry is bad — not so idol worship. An idolator makes a fetish of his idol. An idol worshipper sees God in a stone and, therefore, takes the help of an idol to establish his union with God.... A book, a building, a picture, a carving are, surely, all images in which God does reside, but they are not God. He, who says they are, errs."

✖

" But why pray at all?...God needs no reminder. He is within everyone. Nothing happens without His permission. Our prayer is a heart search. It is a reminder to ourselves that we are helpless without His support. No effort is complete without prayer — without a definite recognition that the best human endeavour is of no effort if it has not God's blessing behind. Prayer is a call to humility. It is a call to self-purification, to inward search."

"God never answers the prayers of the arrogant,
nor the prayers of those who bargain with him."

✗

"There can be no fixed rule laid down as to the time ...
devotional acts should take. It depends upon individual
temperament. These are precious moments in one's daily life.
There are moments when one reviews his immediate past confessing
one's weakness, asks for forgiveness and strength to be and do
better. One minute may be enough for some, twenty-four hours
may be too little for others."

Paramhansa Yogananda records that when bidding the Mahatma goodnight after a long chat at the ashram, he was considerately handed a bottle of citronella oil by him with the words, "The Wardha mosquitoes don't know a thing about ahimsa."

On Ahimsa

"Ahimsa means "non-killing."... It really means that you may not offend anybody; you may not harbour an uncharitable thought, even in connection with one who may consider himself to be your enemy. ... If you express your love — ahimsa — in such a manner that it impresses itself indelibly upon your so-called enemy, he must return that love."

"Non-violence in action cannot be sustained unless it goes hand in hand with non-violence in thought."

"It is no easy thing to walk on the sharp sword-edge of ahimsa in this world which is full of himsa. ... Anger is the enemy of ahimsa; and pride is a monster that swallows it up."

"Hatred injures the hater, never the hated."

"Violence is suicide."

"I [am] 'anti-all-wars'."

"It is the law of love that rules mankind. Had violence, i.e, hate, ruled us we should have become extinct long ago. And yet, the tragedy of it is that the so-called civilised men and nations conduct themselves as if the basis of society was violence."

"Truth and non-violence are no cloistered virtues but are applicable as much in the forum and the legislatures as in the marketplace."

" Ahimsa must express itself through the acts of selfless service of the masses."

" Love, never claims, it ever gives. Love ever suffers, never resents, never revenges itself."

"With patience, good temper and generosity of heart, you will be able to overcome all difficulties. Just as the sea accepts the water of all rivers within itself, purifies it and gives it back again, so you too, if you make yourself as the sea, will be able to accept all people. As the sea makes no distinction between good rivers and bad, but purifies all, so one person, whose heart is purified and enlarged with non-violence and truth, can contain everything in that heart and it will not overflow or lose its serenity."

✗

"If we have no love for our neighbours, no change, however revolutionary, can do us any good."

✗

"It may be long before the law of love will be recognised in international affairs. The machineries of government stand between and hide the hearts of one people from those of another."

"If the mad race for armaments continues, it is bound to result in a slaughter such as has never occurred in history. If there is a victor left the very victory will be a living death for the nation that emerges victorious."

✗

"If we are to reach real peace in this world and if we are to carry on a real war against war, we shall have to begin with children; and if they will grow up in their natural innocence, we won't have to struggle; we won't have to pass fruitless idle resolutions, but we shall go from love to love and peace to peace, until at last all corners of the world are covered with that peace and love for which consciously or unconsciously the whole world is hungering."

✗

"However much I may sympathise with and admire worthy motives, I am an uncompromising opponent of violent methods even to serve the noblest of causes."

Wiping the mist from his old-fashioned spectacles the little man smiled and spoke: "Not yet seven o'clock in the morning – and here's an American journalist to cross-examine me!"

But Mohandas Karamchand Gandhi was wrong – my primary purpose in our interview was not to cross-examine him. I had journeyed to Calcutta because I wanted to experience the astounding magnetism that had made this slight, half-naked man the leader of almost a fifth of the world's population – the 368 millions of India.

—Leonard R.Harris

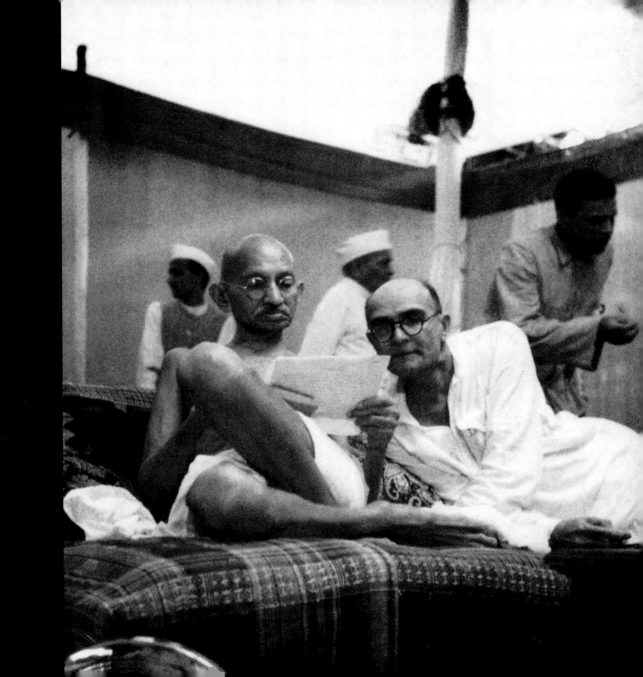

On Satyagraha and Civil Disobedience

"When I read in the 'Sermon on the Mount' such passages as "Resist not him that is evil; but whosoever smiteth thee on thy cheek, turn to him the other also," and "Love your enemies; pray for them that persecute you, that ye may be sons of your Father which is in Heaven," I was simply overjoyed, and found my own opinion confirmed where I least expected it. The 'Bhagwad Gita' deepened the impression, and Tolstoy's 'The Kingdom of God is Within You' gave it a permanent form."

"In the dictionary of satyagraha there is no enemy."

"The satyagrahi strives to reach the reason through the heart,
the method of reaching the heart is to awaken the public opinion."

"A satyagrahi must ceaselessly strive to realise and live truth. And he must never contemplate hurting anyone by thought, word or deed."

"Only he who has mastered the art of obedience to law
knows the art of disobedience to law."

"Satyagraha is a process of educating public opinion, such that it covers all the elements of the society and in the end makes itself irresistible."

"The fight of satyagraha is for the strong in spirit not for the doubter or the timid. Satyagraha teaches us the art of living as well as dying."

"Satyagraha thrives on repression till at last the repressor is tired of it and the object of satyagraha is gained."

"My non-cooperation has its roots not in hatred, but in love."

"Satyagraha can rid society of all evils, political, economic and moral. You are no satyagrahi if you remain silent of passive spectators while your enemy is being done to death."

✕

"My non-cooperation is with methods and systems, never with men."

✕

"Non-cooperation does not in any way mean anarchy or absence of order. For non-cooperation within the State means a closer cooperation among the people themselves. Thus non-cooperation is a process of evolution; it has most aptly been described as evolutionary revolution."

"Non-cooperation, is not a passive state, it is an intensely active state — more active than physical resistance or violence. Passive resistance is a misnomer."

✖

"If our rulers are doing what in our opinion is wrong, and if we feel it our duty to let them hear our advice even though it may be considered sedition, I urge you to speak sedition — but at your peril, you must be prepared to suffer the consequences. And, when you are ready to suffer the consequences and not hit below the belt, then I think you will have made good your right to have your advice heard even by the government."

As the famous Gandhi-Irwin talks concluded, Lord Irwin straightened his tall figure, smiled and inquired whether the Mahatma would not pose with him to commemorate the occasion. The request was politely rejected by Gandhi on the ground that it was his principle never to pose for photographers. The Viceroy, still smiling, invited Gandhi for tea. "Thank you," said Gandhi, unwrapping a paper parcel. "I shall put some of this legalised salt into my tea to remind us of the famous Boston Tea Party".

I want world sympathy in this battle of Right against Might.

Santi

MKGandhi

5ᵗ.4.'30

On India and Independence (Swaraj)

"Independent India, as conceived by me, will have all Indians belonging to different religions living in perfect friendship. There need be no millionaires and no paupers; all would belong to the State, for the State belonged to them. I will die in the act of realising this dream. I would not wish to live to see India torn asunder by civil strife."

"Swaraj is freedom for everyone, the smallest among us, to do as he likes without any physical interference with his liberty."

✗

"Insult offered to a single innocent member of a nation is tantamount to insulting the nation as a whole."

✗

"Our salvation can only come through the farmer. Neither the lawyers, nor the doctors, nor the rich landlords are going to secure it."

"Farmers and workers… make India. Their poverty is India's curse and crime. Their prosperity alone can make India a country fit to live in."

✗

"India must learn to live before she can aspire to die for humanity."

✗

"The pilgrimage to Swaraj is a painful climb…. It means national education, i.e. education of the masses. It means an awakening of national consciousness among the masses. It will not spring like the magician's mango. It will grow almost unperceived like the banyan tree."

"Independence must mean that of the people of India, not of those who are today ruling over them. The rulers should depend on the will of those who are under their heels. Thus, they have to be servants of the people, ready to do their will. Independence must begin at the bottom. . . . Thus, ultimately, it is the individual who is the unit."

✕

"[India] will only then be a truly spiritual nation when we shall show more truth than gold, greater fearlessness than pomp of power and wealth, greater charity than love of self. If we will but cleanse our houses, our palaces and temples of the attributes of wealth and show in them the attributes of morality, we can offer battle to any combinations of hostile forces without having to carry the burden of a heavy militia."

"The youth of a nation to remain a nation must receive all instruction, including the highest, in its own vernaculars… The youth of a nation cannot keep or establish a living contact with the masses unless their knowledge is received and assimilated through a medium understood by the people. Who can calculate the immeasurable loss sustained by the nation, owing to thousands of its young men having been obligated to waste years in mastering a foreign language and its idiom, of which in their daily life they have the least use and in learning which they had to neglect their own mother-tongue and their own literature?"

"Few people realised, few people in the world still realise, that Mahatma Gandhi's laughter was the only relieving factor in his life and he needed to laugh because he was wise, he needed to laugh because he was called upon to bear the world's burden. Everyone went to him, to consult him, to ask his help, to lay their burden on his already burdened shoulders. He refused no one. Even a child that went to him found him full of humour and fun and went away fully satisfied. He gave counsel to those who had the destiny of the whole country in their hands. He talked to strangers and to friends and no stranger remained a stranger in the first moment of coming in his presence."

—Sarojini Naidu

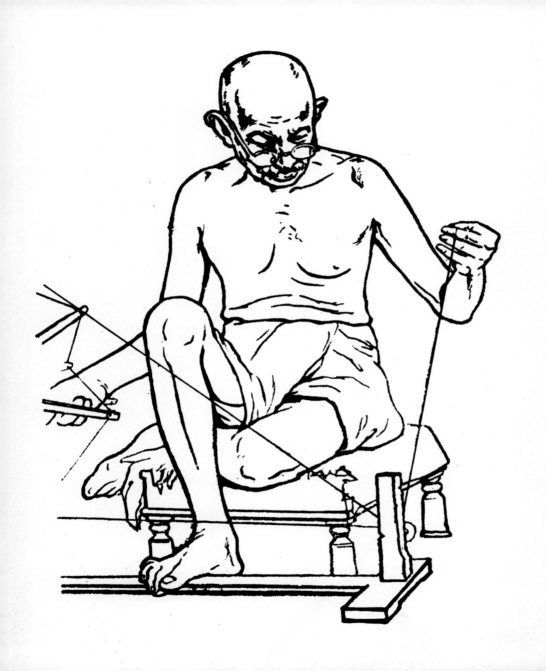

On Action, Duty and Service

"Action for one's own self binds,
action for the sake of others delivers from bondage."

"Thought is never complete unless it finds expression
in action and action limits your thought."

✗

"Mere brave speech without action is letting off useless steam."

✗

"You must be the change you wish to see in the world."

✗

"What distinguished the man from the brute is his conscious
striving to realise the spirit within."

"Rights accrue automatically to him who duly performs his duties. In fact the right to perform one's duties is the only right that is worth living for and dying for. It covers all legitimate rights. All the rest is garb under one guise or another and contains in it the seed of ahimsa."

✗

"One who would sacrifice his life for others has hardly time to reserve for himself a place in the sun."

✗

"My ahimsa would not tolerate the idea of giving a free meal to a healthy person who has not worked for it in some honest way."

✗

"We dare not enter the kingdom of liberty with mere lip-homage to truth and non-violence."

"Put your talents in the service of the country instead of converting them into pounds, shillings and pence."

"The propagation of truth and non-violence can be done less by books than by actually living on those principles."

"Service can have no meaning unless one takes pleasure in it. When it is done for show or for fear of public opinion, it stunts the man and crushes his spirit. Service which is rendered without joy helps neither the servant nor the served. But all other pleasures and possessions pale into nothingness before service which is rendered in a spirit of joy."

"Personal service when it merges into universal service
is the only service worth doing."

✗

"My life is dedicated to the service of Indians through the religion of
non-violence, which I believe to be the root of Hinduism."

✗

"One's life is not a single straight line; it is a bundle of duties very
often conflicting. And one is called upon continually to make
one's choice between one duty and another."

"Gandhi was a great Indian nationalist, but at the same time he was a leader of international stature. His teachings and his actions have left a deep impression on millions of people."

—President Truman

On Reform, Leadership and Resolution

"Discontent is a very useful thing. As long as a man is contented with his present lot, so long is it difficult to persuade him to come out of it. Therefore it is that every reform must be preceded by discontent."

"We won't find the remedy for human ills by losing patience and by rejecting everything that is old because it is old. Our ancestors also dreamed, perhaps vaguely, the same dreams that fire us with zeal."

"To give a little bit of money is easy enough, to do a little thing one's self is more difficult."

"No matter how insignificant the thing you have to do, do it as well as you can, give it as much of your care and attention as you would give to the thing you regard as most important."

"Those who want to do good are not selfish, they are not in a hurry, they know that to impregnate people with good requires a long time. But evil has wings."

✗

"Courage, endurance, fearlessness and above all self-sacrifice are the qualities of our leaders."

✗

"We should be ashamed of resting or having a square meal so long as there is one able-bodied man or woman without work or food."

"The taking of a vow does not mean that we are able to observe it completely from the very beginning; it does mean constant and honest effort in thought, word and deed with a view to its fulfillment. We must not practice self-deception by resorting to some make-believe."

"Pledges and vows are, and should be, taken on rare occasions. A man who takes a vow every now and then is sure to stumble."

"One never can achieve anything lasting in this world by being irresolute."

"Begin with a Charter of Duties of Man and I promise the rights will follow as spring follows winter. I write from experience. As a young man I began life by seeking to assert my rights and I soon discovered I had none not even over my wife. So I began by discovering and performing my duty by my wife, my children, friends, companions and society and I find today that I have greater rights, perhaps than any living man I know. If this is too tall a claim then I say I do not know anyone who possesses greater rights than I."

✖

"A voice in the wilderness has a potency which voices uttered in the midst of 'the madding crowd' lack. For, the voice in the wilderness has meditation, deliberation, and unquenchable faith behind it, whilst the babble of voices has generally nothing, but the backing of the experience of personal enjoyment."

Some teachers of the National College in Mumbai on a visit to Ahmedabad during their Diwali holidays saw Mahatma Gandhi and asked him for advice as to how they should best spend the vacation.

He was observing silence that day and thus wrote the following answer on a piece of paper:

> Card, Spin, Weave,
> Spin, Weave, Card,
> Weave, Card, Spin.

On reading the reply, the teachers burst out laughing. One of them took the piece of paper to keep it as a memento.

On Education
and the Arts

"Knowledge which stops at the head and does not penetrate into the heart is of but little use in the critical times of living experience."

"It is not literacy or learning that make a man, but education for real life. What would it matter if [men] knew everything but did not know how to live in brotherliness with their neighbours?"

✗

"There is something radically wrong in the system of education that fails to arm girls and boys to fight against social or other evils. That education alone is of value which draws out the faculties of a student, so as to enable him or her to solve correctly the problems of life in every apartment."

✗

"It is a sign of national degradation when little children are removed from schools and are employed in earning wages. No nation worthy of the name can possibly afford so to misuse her children. At least up to the age of sixteen they must be kept in schools. Students must become pioneers in conservative reform, conserving all that is good in the nation and fearlessly ridding society of the innumerable abuses that have crept into it."

"Language is at best an imperfect medium of expression. No man can fully express in words what he feels or thinks."

✗

"The education of the heart … can [not] be imparted through books. It can only be done through the living touch of the teacher."

✗

"The teachers' work lies more outside than inside the lecture room."

✗

"Literary training by itself adds not an inch to one's moral height and character-building is independent of literary training."

"Physical training should have as much
place in the curriculum as mental training."

✖

"We have up to now concentrated on stuffing children's minds with all kinds
of information, without ever thinking of stimulating and developing them."

✖

"I have no university education worth the name. My high school
career was never above average. I was thankful if I could pass my
examinations. Distinction in the school was beyond my aspiration."

✖

"Music has given me peace. I can remember occasions when music
instantly tranquilised my mind, when I was greatly agitated over
something. Music has helped me to overcome anger."

"To me, art, in order to be truly great must, like the beauty of Nature, be universal in its appeal, it must be simple in its presentation and direct in its expression, like the language of Nature."

✖

"To a true artist only that face is beautiful which, quite apart from its exterior, shines with the truth within the soul."

✖

"All true art is the expression of the soul. The outward forms have value only in so far as they are the expression of the inner spirit of man. ... I know that many call themselves artists in whose work there is absolutely no trace of the soul's upward urge and unrest. ... All true art must help the soul realise its inner self."

Verrier Elwin, once went to see Gandhi when he was staying with a high-caste Indian lady. For reason of caste she did not wish to offer Elwin hospitality, but would not admit the real reason, which Gandhi immediately recognised. She said she had no spare room. Gandhi said the verandah would do. But what about his bath, asked the lady.

"He doesn't bathe," said Gandhi, beginning to enjoy himself.

"And the toilet...?"

The reply was shattering. "Oh, Verrier sublimates everything."

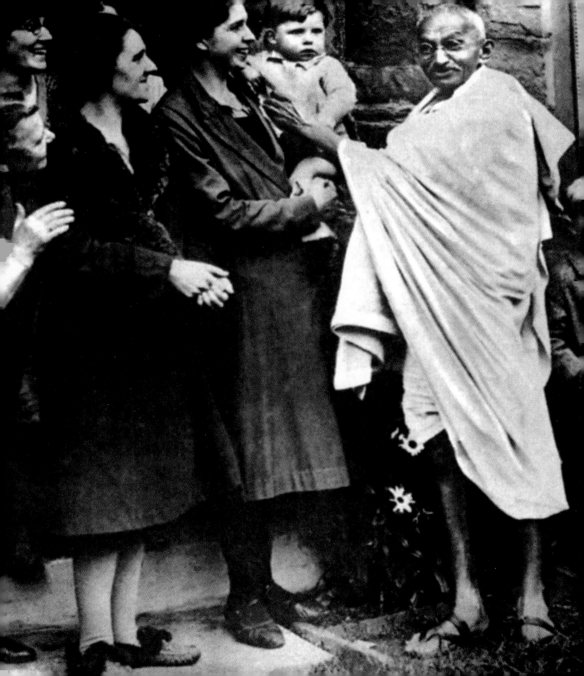

On Equality and Tolerance

"In the eyes of God, who is the creator of all, His creatures are all equal. Had he made any distinctions of high and low between man and man, they would have been visible as are the distinctions between say, an elephant and an ant. But he has endowed all human beings impartially with the same shape and the same natural wants...it can never be an act of merit to look down upon any human beings as inferior to us."

"Assumption of superiority by any person over any other is a sin against God and man. Thus caste, in so far as it connotes distinctions in status, is an evil."

✘

"If we could erase the 'It's' and the 'Mine's' from religion, politics, economics, etc., we shall soon be free and bring heaven upon earth."

✘

"The golden rule of conduct is mutual toleration, seeing that we will never all think alike and we shall see Truth in fragments and from different angles of vision. Conscience is not the same thing for all. Whilst, therefore, it is a good guide for individual conduct, imposition of that conduct upon all will be an insufferable interference with everybody's freedom of conscience."

"Some think of removing physical untouchability, some talk of the removal of the so-called untouchables' disabilities with regard to the use of public wells, schools and temples. But you should go much further. You should love them even as yourselves, so that the moment they see you they might feel that you are one of them."

"To my mind the life of a lamb is no less precious than that of a human being. I should be unwilling to take the life of a lamb for the sake of the human body. I hold that, the more helpless a creature, the more entitled it is to protection by man from cruelty of man."

"Ruskin's 'Unto This Last' … was impossible to lay aside, once I had begun it. It gripped me. … I determined to change my life in accordance with the ideals of the book. … [It] brought about an instantaneous and practical transformation in my life. … The teachings of 'Unto This Last' I understood to be: 1. That the good of the individual is contained in the good of all. 2. That a lawyer's work has the same value as the barber's in as much as all have the same right of earning their livelihood from their work. 3. That a life of labour, the life of the tiller of the soil and the handicraftsman, is the life worth living. … I arose with the dawn, ready to reduce these principles to practice."

"If Gandhism is another name for sectarianism, it deserves to be destroyed. If I were to know, after my death, that what I stood for had degenerated into sectarianism, I should be deeply pained. Let no one say that he is a follower of Gandhi. You are no followers but fellow students, fellow pilgrims, fellow seekers, fellow workers."

✗

"I do not believe in caste in the modern sense.
It is an excrescence and a handicap on progress."

"All the while we were talking, my son Rajiv, then three and a half years old, played with the flowers decorating Gandhi. Sometimes he would slip the jasmine veni on his feet like an anklet. Sometimes he would hand it on his big toe…. He laughed and joked and was full of fun. Little did we guess that we would never see his wide toothless smile again, nor feel the glow of his protection."

— Indira Gandhi

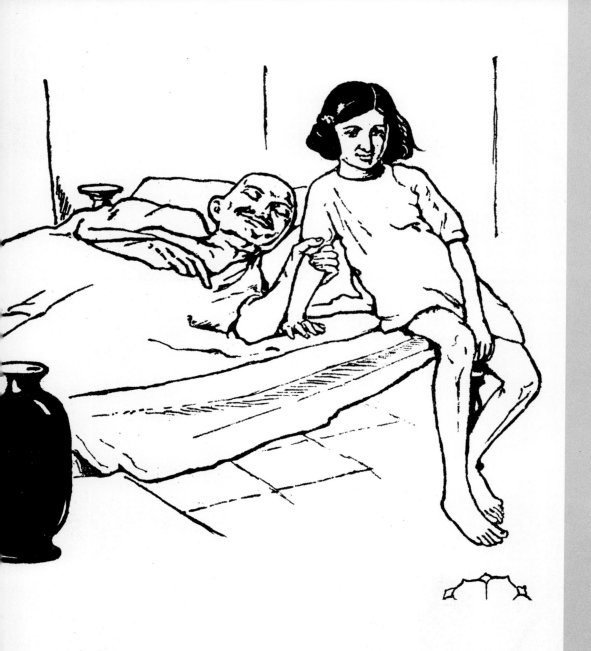

On Women

"If only the women of the world would come together
they could display such heroic non-violence as to kick
away the atom bomb like a mere ball... If the women of Asia
wake up, they will dazzle the world."

“Men can never be a woman’s equal in the spirit of selfless service with which nature has endowed her.”

“Man is born of woman; he is flesh of her flesh and bone of her bone.”

“I have worshipped women as the living embodiment of the spirit of service and sacrifice.”

“Woman is more fitted than man to make explorations and take bolder action in ahimsa.”

"In a plan of life based on non-violence, woman has as much
right to shape her own destiny as man has to shape his."

✗

"Woman is the companion of man, gifted with equal mental capacities.
She has the right to participate in the minutest details in the activities of
man, and she has an equal right of freedom and liberty with him."

✗

"If we would be pure, if we would save Hinduism, we must rid
ourselves of this poison of enforced widowhood."

✗

"More is always expected from those who give much."

"Any young man who makes a dowry a condition of marriage, discredits his education and his country and dishonours womanhood.... A strong public opinion should be created in condemnation of the degrading practice of dowry, and young men, who soil their fingers with such ill-gotten gold, should be excommunicated from society. Parents of girls should cease to be dazzled by English degrees, and should not hesitate to travel outside their little castes and provinces to secure true gallant men for their daughters."

�֍

"If non-violence is the law of our being, the future is with the woman."

"Hindu culture has erred on the side of the excessive subordination of the wife to the husband, and has insisted on the complete merging of the wife in the husband. This has resulted in the husband, sometimes, usurping and exercising authority that reduces him to the level of the brute."

"Men to be men must be able to trust their womenfolk, even as the latter are compelled to trust them."

"I was quite unprepared to meet such a loveable old man, with a warm, human manner, great good humour, charming manners, and perhaps most unexpectedly of all, an unfailing sense of humour."

—Lord Mountbatten

On Man, Nature and Civilisation

"You must not lose faith in humanity. Humanity is an ocean. If a few drops of the ocean are dirty, the ocean does not become dirty."

"Man will ever remain imperfect, and it will always be his part to try and be perfect. Perfection in love or non-possession will remain an unattainable ideal as long as we are alive, but towards which we must ceaselessly strive."

✗

"I have discovered that man is superior to the system he propounds."

✗

"The truest test of civilisation, culture and dignity is character and not clothing."

✗

"Human society is a ceaseless growth, an unfoldment in terms of spirituality."

✗

"If you have no character to lose, people will have no faith in you."

"Civilisation is that mode of conduct which points out to man the path of duty. Performance of duty and observance of morality are convertible terms. To observe morality is to attain mastery over our mind and our passions. So doing, we know ourselves."

"It is beneath human dignity to lose one's individuality and become a mere cog in the machine."

"What will tell in the end will be character and not knowledge of letters."

"If I am true to myself, if I am true to mankind, if I am true to humanity, I must understand all faults that human flesh is heir to."

"You are a strange man, Mr.Gandhi! You are so sincere, you embarrass us; so simple, you baffle me."

—Louise Housman

On Personal Ethics

"To say what offends another is against Ethics and certainly against spirituality if the saying is not required in the interest of truth."

"Trivialities possess deadly potentialities."

"The most practical, the most dignified way of going on in the world is to take people at their word, when you have no positive reason to the contrary."

"The world learns to apply to a man the standards which he applies to himself."

"I preach against the modern artificial life of sensual enjoyment, and ask men and women to go back to the simple life. . . . Without an intelligent return to simplicity, there is no escape from our descent to a state lower than brutality."

"There is no question of loin-cloth civilisation. The adoption of the loin-cloth was for me a necessity. But in so far as the loin-cloth also spells simplicity let it represent Indian civilisation."

✕

"It has always been a mystery to me how men can feel themselves honoured by the humiliation of their fellow-beings."

✕

"The motive will determine the quality of the act."

✕

"It is discipline and restraint that separate us from the brute. If we will be men walking with our heads erect, and not walking on all fours, let us understand and put ourselves under voluntary discipline and restraint."

"Why are you so uncharitable to those who drink?" asked an English student of Gandhi when the latter was in London, towards the close of 1931.

"Because I am charitable to those who suffer from the effects of the curse," Gandhi replied.

On Health and Diet

"If we knew all the laws of nature or having known, had, the power to obey them in thought, word and deed, we would be God Himself and not need to do anything at all. As it is, we hardly know the laws and have little power to obey them. Hence, disease and all its effects. It is, therefore, enough for us to realise that every illness is but a breach of some unknown law of nature and to strive to know the laws and pray for power to obey. Heart prayer, therefore, whilst we are ill, is both work and medicine."

"It is far easier and safer to prevent illness by the observance of the laws of health than to set about curing the illness which has been brought on by our own ignorance and carelessness."

✗

"Illness is the result not only of our actions but also of our thoughts."

✗

"The relation between the body and the mind is so intimate that, if either of them got out of order, the whole system would suffer. Hence it follows that a pure character is the foundation of health in the real sense of the term; and . . . all evil thoughts and evil passions are but different forms of disease."

✗

"Our aim should be to attain the maximum of health by all legitimate means; we should not be content merely to live anyhow."

"Our passion for exercise should become so strong that we could not bring ourselves to dispense with it on all account. We hardly realise how weak and futile is our mental work when unaccompanied by hard physical exercise."

✗

"Cigars and cigarettes, whether foreign or indigenous, must be avoided. Cigarette smoking is like an opiate, and the cigars that you smoke have a touch of opium about them. They get to your nerves and you cannot leave them afterwards. How can a single [person] foul his mouth by converting it into a chimney?"

✗

"If it is necessary to take coffee or tea to keep awake, let them not drink coffee, or tea but go to sleep. We must not become slaves to these things. But the majority of the people, who drink coffee or tea, are slaves to them."

"True happiness is impossible without true health and true health is impossible without a rigid control of the palate."

✗

"It is impossible to lay down hard and fast rules in the matter of food. . . . Although, however, it is impossible to say conclusively what sort of food we should eat, it is the clear duty of every individual to bestow serious thought on the matter."

✗

"There is a great deal of truth in the saying that man becomes what he eats. The grosser the food, the grosser the body."

✗

"More people are weak through overfeeding or wrong feeding than through underfeeding. It is wonderful, if we chose the right diet, what extraordinary small quantity would suffice."

"The man who eats to live, who is friends with the five powers-earth, water, ether, sun and air and who is a servant of god, the creator of all of these, ought not to fall ill."

✗

"Harbour impurity of mind and body and you have untruth and violence in you."

✗

"My dislike for medicines steadily increased.... I believe that man has little need to drug himself. Nine hundred and ninety-nine cases out of a thousand can be brought round by means of a well-regulated diet, water and earth treatment and similar household remedies. He who runs to the doctor...for every little ailment, and swallows all kinds of vegetable and mineral drugs, not only curtails his life, but, by becoming the slave of his body instead of remaining its master, loses self control, and ceases to be a man."

"Warrior, prophet, saint."

—G.D.Birla

"…one of the greatest men of human history. He stands alone."

—Pearl S.Buck

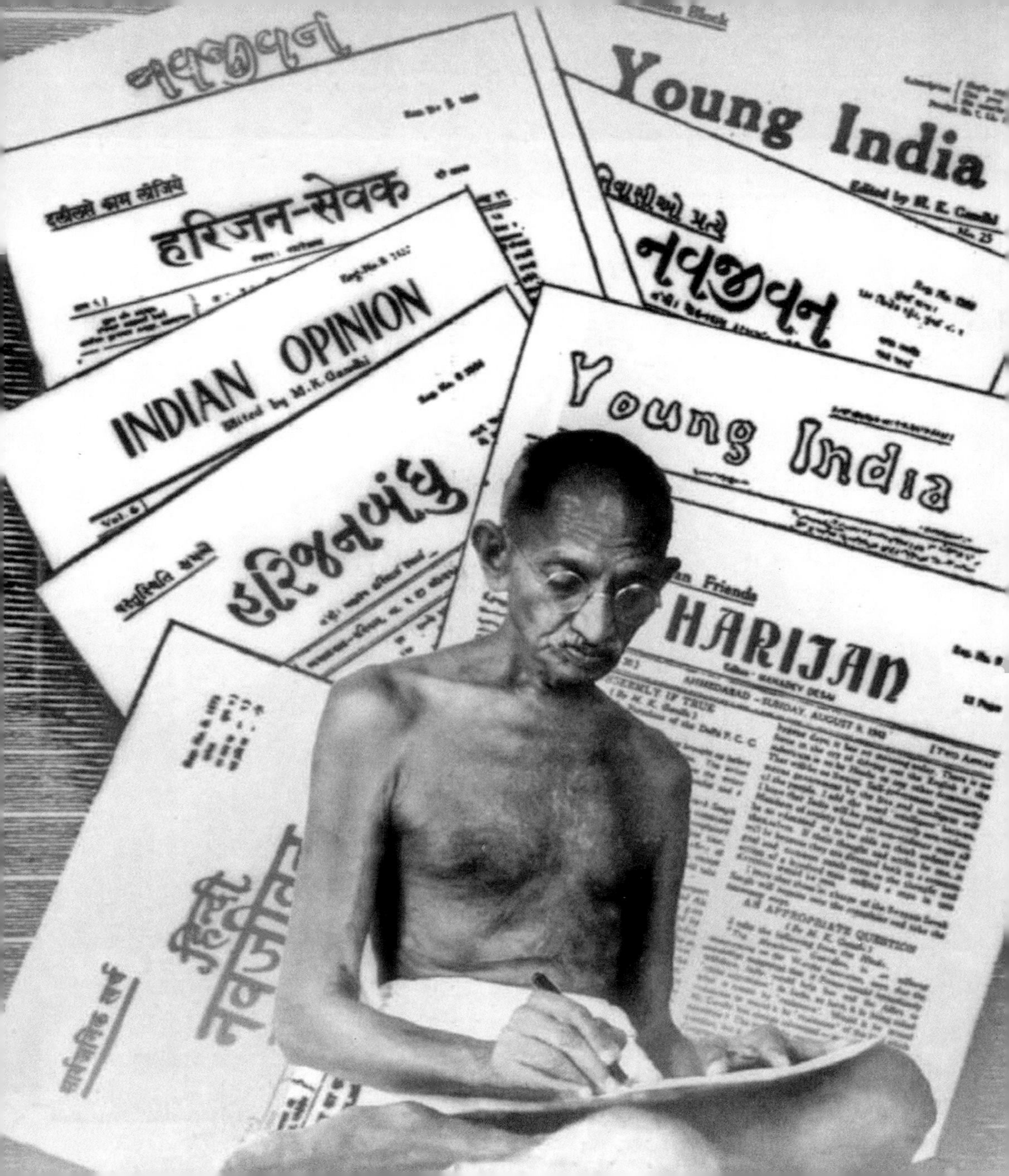

Young India
हरिजन-सेवक
INDIAN OPINION
Young India
HARIJAN

On Resilience

"*What a good thing is silence! … The joy one derives from silence is unique. How good it will be, if everyone observed silence for sometime everyday! Silence is not for some great men; I know that whatever one person is able to do can be done by everyone, given the effort. There is a saying amongst us that through silence everything can be achieved. There is much truth in this saying.*"

"Silence is a great help to a seeker after truth. In the attitude of silence the soul finds the path in a clearer light and what is elusive and deceptive resolves itself into crystal clearness. Our life is a long and arduous quest after Truth, and the soul requires inward restfulness to attain its full height."

"I wanted to rest for one day a week. So I instituted the day of silence. Later of course I clothed it with all kinds of virtues and gave it a spiritual cloak. But the motivation was really nothing more than that I wanted to have a day off. . . . Silence is very relaxing. It is not relaxing in itself. But when you can talk and don't, it gives you great relief – and there is time for thought."

"A calm reflection will show that all sins like lying, cheating and stealing are ultimately due to our subjection to the palate. He who is able to control the palate will easily be able to control the senses."

"Most of my reading since 1893 has been done in jail."

"Jail is jail for thieves and bandits. For me it is a palace."

"My friends need not be at all anxious about me. I am as happy as a bird. And I do not feel that I am accomplishing less here than outside the prison. My stay here is a good school for me, and my separation from my fellow workers should prove whether our movement is an independently evolving organism or merely the work of one individual and, therefore, something very transient."

✕

"We have here [in Yervada prison] learned to recognise friends among animals. We have a cat, who is a revelation. And if we had vision enough, we should appreciate the language of trees and plants and value their friendship."

"A "full" meal is . . . a crime against God and man – the latter because the full-mealers deprive their neighbors of their portion. God's economy provides from day to day just enough food for all in just medicinal doses. We are all of the tribe of full-mealers. Instinctively, to know the medicinal dose required is a Herculean task, for by parental training we are gluttons. Then, when it is almost too late, it dawns upon some of us that food is made not to enjoy but to sustain the body as our slave. It becomes from that moment a grim fight against inherited and acquired habit of eating for pleasure. Hence the necessity for a complete fast at intervals and partial fasts forever."

People from far and wide wrote to Gandhi. No matter what the address, the letters reached Gandhi. One letter had a picture of him cut out from a newspaper, with 'London' written below. In India, as Mahadev Desai, Gandhi's private secretary recounts in his diary, once a letter came from Austria with only 'Bapu' written on it. The Indian Dead Letter Office wrote 'Shri Bapu, that is Mahatma Gandhi, Yervada Central Prison' and it reached Bapu. A quaint postal envelope addressed to "King of India, Mahatma Gandhi, Delhi' was redirected quite correctly to Yervada Jail. Another envelope carried a picture of Gandhi, with only the word 'to' above it and it reached him. An envelope from America with a picture of Gandhi and the word 'India' written underneath it also arrived at Gandhi's doorstep. An Indian once wrote to Gandhi, on the envelope he wrote in Hindi, 'Mahatma Gandhi, Jahan hon Vahah' (wherever he is) and the letter came to Wardha.

GANDHIJI'S TEN COMMANDMENTS

On Himself

"I lay claim to nothing exclusively divine in me. I do not claim prophetship. I am but a humble seeker after truth and bent upon finding it. I count no sacrifice too great for the sake of seeing God face to face. The whole of my activity whether it may be called social, political, humanitarian or ethical is directed to that end. As I know that God is found more often in the lowliest of His creatures than in the high and mighty, I am struggling to reach the status of these. I cannot render this service without entering politics, I find myself in them. Thus I am no master, I am but a struggling, erring, humble servant of India and therein, of humanity."

"I am, indeed, a practical dreamer. My dreams are not airy nothings. I want to convert my dreams into realities, as far as possible."

"I am not a visionary. I claim to be a practical idealist."

"Cranks, faddists and madmen often find their way to the Ashram – and I am the maddest of them all."

"All my life through, the very insistence on truth has taught me to appreciate the beauty of compromise.... It has often meant endangering my life and incurring the displeasure of friends. But truth is hard as adamant and tender as a blossom."

"I assure all my admirers and friends that they will please me better if they will forget the Mahatma and remember Gandhiji… or think of me simply as Gandhi."

✗

"Even [the bully] is entitled to justice, for immediately you brush aside the bully and be unjust to him, you justify his bullying."

✗

"If all laboured for their bread and no more, then there would be enough food and enough leisure for all. Then there would be no cry for overpopulation, no disease and no such misery as we see around. Such labour will be the highest form of sacrifice. Men will no doubt do many other things either through their bodies or through their minds, but all this will be a labour of love for the common good. There will then be no rich and no poor, none high and none low, no touchable and no untouchable. This may be an unattainable ideal. But we need not, therefore, cease to strive for it. … We should eat to live, not live to eat."

"I want the cultures of all lands to be blown about my house as freely as possible. But I refuse to be blown off my feet by any."

✂

"I must admit my many inconsistencies. Since I am called 'Mahatma,' I might well endorse Emerson's saying that 'foolish consistency is the hobgoblin of little minds'."

✂

"The word 'saint' should be ruled out of present life. It is too sacred a word to be lightly applied to anybody, much less to one like myself who claims only to be a humble searcher after Truth, knows his limitations, makes mistakes, never hesitates to admit them and frankly confesses that he, like a scientist, is making experiments about some 'of the eternal verities' of life, but cannot even claim to be a scientist because he can show no tangible proof of scientific accuracy in his methods or such tangible results of his experiments as modern science demands."

"Never take anything for gospel truth even if it comes from a Mahatma unless it appeals to both … head and heart."

✕

"Often the title [Mahatma] has deeply pained me; and there is not a moment I can recall when it may be said to have tickled me."

✕

"We are thieves in a way. If I take anything that I do not need for my own immediate use, and keep it, I thieve it from somebody else. It is the fundamental law of Nature, without exception, that Nature produces enough for our wants from day to day, and if only everybody took enough for himself and nothing more, there would be no more pauperism in this world, there would be no man dying from starvation in this world. … I do not want to dispossess anybody. … If somebody else possesses more than I do, let him. But as far as my own life has to be regulated, I do say that I dare not possess anything which I do not want. You and I have no right to anything that we really have until [the] millions are clothed and fed better. You and I, who ought to know better, must adjust our wants, and even undergo voluntary starvation in order that they may be nursed, fed and clothed."

"In every century there are only three or four great men whose influence bestrides the world during their lifetime. Mr.Gandhi was one of these."

—*Evening Standard*

On Discrimination

"I lived in South Africa for twenty years, but never once thought of going to see the diamond mines there, partly because I was afraid lest as an 'untouchable' I should be refused admission and insulted."

"The train reached Martizburg, the capital of Natal [South Africa], at about 9 P.M.... A passenger came next and looked me up and down. He saw that I was a 'coloured' man.... Another official came to me and said, "Come along, you must go the van compartment." "But I have a first class ticket," said I. "That doesn't matter", rejoined the other...."You must leave this compartment, or else I shall have to call a police constable to push you out." "Yes, you may. I refuse to get out voluntarily."The constable came. He took me by the hand and pushed me out. ... I refused to go the other compartment and the train steamed away."

✕

"I applied for admission as an advocate of the Supreme Court [of Natal]. ... The Law Society now sprang a surprise on me by serving me with a notice opposing my application for admission. ... The main objection was that, when the regulations regarding admission of advocates were made, the possibility of a coloured man applying could not have been contemplated."

"Mr. Ellerthorpe invited me to the Bengal Club [of Calcutta] where he was staying. He did not realise that an Indian could not be taken to the drawing room of the Club. ... He expressed his sorrow regarding this prejudice of the local Englishmen and apologised to me for not having been able to take me to the drawing room."

✖

"I once went to an English hair-cutter in Pretoria. He contemptuously refused to cut my hair. I certainly felt hurt, but immediately purchased a pair of clippers and cut my hair before the mirror. I succeeded more or less in cutting the front hair, but I spoiled the back. The friends in court shook with laughter. "What's wrong with your hair, Gandhi? Rats have been at it?" "No, the white barber would not condescend to touch my black hair."

✖

"I reached Johannesburg quite safely that night. ... Taking a cab I asked to be driven to the Grand National Hotel. I saw the manager and asked for a room. He eyed me for a moment, and politely saying, "I am very sorry, we are full up," bade me good-bye."

"And then the laughter died suddenly with three shots from a revolver at Delhi, and we were all ashamed."

—Reginald Reynolds

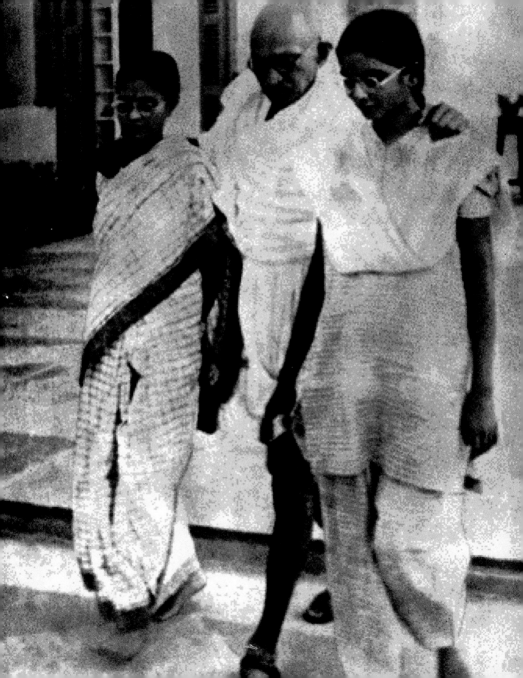

"The odd thing about assassins, Dr. King, is that they think they've killed you."

On Death and

Assassination

"I keep no bodyguard to protect me.

My chest is literally bare."

"What new message can I give you at the age of 68? And where is the use of my giving you a message if you pass a resolution there of assassinating me or burning my effigy? Assassinating the body of course does not matter, for out of my ashes a thousand Gandhis will arise. But what if you assassinate or burn the principles I have lived for?"

✗

"I am a born fighter who does not know failure."

✗

"Death is as necessary for man's growth as life itself."

"My writings should be cremated with my body. What I have done will endure, not what I have said and written."

"For many years I have accorded intellectual assent to the proposition that death is only a big chance in life and nothing more, and should be welcome when it arrives. I have deliberately made a supreme attempt to cast out from my heart all fear whatsoever including the fear of death. Still I remember occasions in my life when I have not rejoiced at the thought of approaching death as one might rejoice at the prospect of meeting a long lost friend. Thus man often remains weak notwithstanding all his efforts to be strong."

"We really live through and in our work. We perish through our perishable bodies, if instead of using them as temporary instruments, we identify ourselves with them.... Sorrow over separation and death is perhaps the greatest delusion. To realise that it is a delusion is to become free. There is no death, no separation of the substance. And yet the tragedy of it is that though we love friends for the substance we recognise in them, we deplore the destruction of the insubstantial that covers the substance for the time being."

'If I am to die by the bullet of a madman, I must do so smiling. There must be no anger within me. God must be in my heart and on my lips. And you [Rajkumari Amrit Kaur] promise me one thing. Should such a thing happen, you are not to shed one tear."

Last words before assassination: He, Ram! He, Ram!

"So, it is all over.

The world feels so empty. Dreadfully empty.

The bird escaped at 5 p.m. on Friday, 30th January.

The body remained with us and the lingering smile on the face kept on the illusion going for some time."

—C. Rajagopalachari

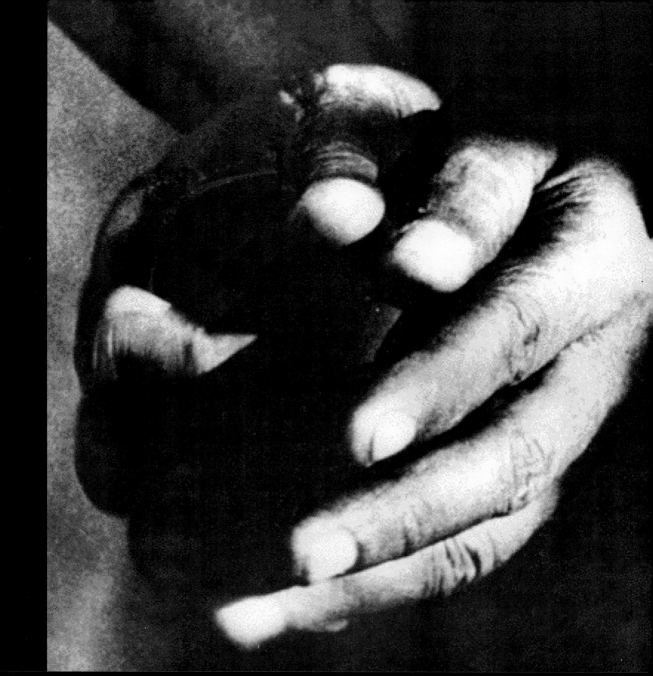

Biographical Chronology

1869
2 Oct
Mohandas Karamchand Gandhi was born into a Vaishya family at Porbander in Kathiawar, Gujarat; the youngest of three sons of Karamchand Gandhi, Prime Minister in Porbander, Rajkot, and Vanakner States, and his fourth wife Putlibai.

1876
Goes to Rajkot with parents; attends primary school there until twelfth year. Betrothal to Kasturbai, daughter of Gokuldas Makanji.

1882
Marries Kasturbai Makanji.

1888
Spring
Birth of Harilal.
4 Sept
Despite disapproval of caste elders, sails for England to study.

1890
19 Sept
Executive member of the London Vegetarian Society

1891
10 June
Called to the Bar and enrols in the High Court of London.
12 June
Sails for India.

1892
Spring
Birth of Manilal.
14 May
Receives permission to practise law in Kathiawar. Fails to establish successful practise. Settles in Rajkot as legal draughtsman.

1893
Apr
Sails for South Africa as legal advisor to Dada Abdullah & Company.

June

Ordered off train to Pretoria. Makes resolve to resist racial discrimination non-violently.

1894

22 Aug

Organises Natal Indian Congress

3 Sept

Enrolled as barrister in the High Courts of Natal and the Transvaal over opposition of European lawyers.

1895

May

Appeals to Natal Assembly and to Lord Ripon against re-indenture clause in Indian Immigration Bill.

16 Dec

Issues *The Indian Franchise: An Appeal to Every Briton in South Africa*.

1896

5 June

Sails for India.

June

Addresses meetings on behalf of Indians in South Africa.

30 Nov

Sails for South Africa with his family.

1897

May

Birth of Ramdas.

1898

Petitions local and Imperial authorities regarding discriminatory laws.

1900

May 22

Birth of Devadas.

1901

18 Oct

Sails with family to India.

27 Dec

Offers resolution on South Africa at Indian National Congress.

1902
20 Nov
Returns with family to South Africa in response to call to champion Indian cause against anti-Asiatic legislation in the Transvaal.

1903
Feb
Enrols as Attorney of Supreme Court of the Transvaal. Opens law office in Johannesburg.
4 June
Launches *Indian Opinion*.

1905
May
Begins learning Tamil.
9 Aug
Calls for revision of Bill levying poll tax against Natal Indians.
19 Aug
Calls for united opposition to Bengal partition and supports boycott of British goods.

1906
12 May
Advocates Home Rule for India.
Sept 11
Addresses mass meeting of Indians at Empire Theatre in Johannesburg calling for withdrawal of Asiatic Registration Bill.
3 Oct
Sails for England to seek redress from British government.
7 Nov
Addresses members of Parliament.
Dec
Returns to South Africa.

1907
14 July
Calls upon Indians not to re-register.
31 July
Explains significance of Passive Resistance. General Strike follows.
28 Dec
Conducts his own trial and appears in defence of pickets; ordered to leave Transvaal within

forty eight hours. Later, speaks at meeting in Government Square.

1908
10 Jan
Adopts term 'Satyagraha' in place of 'Passive Resistance'.
Sentenced to two months' imprisonment. Released on 31 January along with all other Satyagrahis.
10 Feb
Assaulted and nearly killed by Mir Alam Khan and other Pathans.
Appeals from his sick-bed that assailants be forgiven, and asks Asiatics to give their finger-prints voluntarily.
16 Aug
Addresses mass meeting and encourages the burning of registration certificates.
23 Aug
Mass meeting in Johannesburg in which more registration certificates are burnt. Mir Alam, Gandhi's assailant, and other Pathans admit their error and resolve 'to fight to the end'.

1909
23 June
Sails for England.
10 July
Arrives in London. With assistance of Lord Ampthill, seeks to educate influential British leaders.
13 Nov
Returns to South Africa. En route writes *Hind Swaraj* and translates Tolstoy's '*Letter to a Hindoo*'.

1911
22 Apr
Smuts agrees to assurances demanded by Indians in reciprocation of suspension of Satyagraha Movement.

1912
22 Oct
Gokhale arrives in Cape Town. Gandhi accompanies him during a five-week tour. Gives up European dress and milk and restricts his diet to fresh and dried fruit.

1913

Apr

Kasturbai joins the Satyagraha.

15 Sept

Satyagraha is revived. Party of twelve men and four women, including Kasturbai Gandhi, leave Durban for Volksrust.

23 Sept

Kasturbai is arrested along with other satyagrahis. Sentenced to three months' imprisonment at hard labour.

28 Oct

Leads march from Newcastle with 1,700 satyagrahis.

1914

13 Jan

Begins negotiations with General Smuts.

22 Jan

Suspends Satyagraha following agreement with Smuts.

18 July

Sails for London en route to India, leaving South Africa for the last time.

8 Aug

Given reception at Hotel Cecil by English and Indian friends; Jinnah, Lala Lajpat Rai, Sarojini Naidu are among those present.

19 Dec

Owing to ill health sails for India.

1915

9 Jan

Arrival in Bombay. Awarded Kaiser-i-Hind Gold Medal for ambulance services.

20 May

Establishes Satyagraha Ashram (later known as Sabarmati Ashram) at Ahmedabad.

Sept

Admits untouchable family to Satyagraha Ashram.

1916

Tours India and Burma, travelling third class on railway.

21 Oct

At Bombay Provincial Conference held at Ahmedabad, Gandhi proposes election of Jinnah as President.

26 Dec

Attends Indian National Congress at Lucknow.

29 Dec

Presides over All-India Common Script and
   Common Language Conference in Lucknow.

1917

Idea of using spinning wheel to produce
   handmade cloth on large scale takes root in
   his mind.

1918

20 Feb

   Presides over annual gathering of Bhagini
   Samaj in Bombay, speaking on women's
   education.

22 Feb

Leads Satyagraha campaign on behalf of mill
   workers in Ahmedabad. Settlement reached
   on 18 March.

27 Apr

Attends Viceroy's War conference at Delhi,
   addressing it in Hindustani. Tours to raise
   recruits for British armed forces.

14 Nov

Opening of the Gujarati Swadeshi store.

1919

24 Feb

Notifies Viceroy of Satyagraha Pledge.

Mar

Issues first 'Satyagraha leaflet', quoting Thoreau.

6 Apr

Inaugurates all India Satyagraha movement:
   countrywide hartal.

7 Apr

First issue of *Satyagrahi* released without
   registration.

10-12 Apr

Arrested on the way to Delhi for refusal to
   comply with order not to enter the Punjab.
   Outbreaks of violence in several towns
   accompany his escort back to Bombay.

13 Apr

Massacre at Amritsar.

14 Apr

Commencement of 3 day penitential fast. Leads
   Satyagraha campaign against the Rowlatt Act.

Confesses his Himalayan Miscalculation regarding mass Satyagraha. Martial law declared in Punjab.

18 Apr
Suspends Satyagraha.

Sept
Assumes editorship of *Navajivan*.

Oct
Assumes editorship of *Young India*.

24 Nov
Presides over All-India Khilafat Conference at Delhi.

1920

2 Apr
Rabindranath Tagore visits Sabarmati Ashram.

1 Aug
Addresses letter to Viceroy, returning Kaiser-i-Hind, Zulu War and Boer War medals.

31 Aug
Takes pledge to wear Khadi for life.

8 Sept
Special session of Indian National Congress accepts his programme of non-cooperation to secure redress of Punjab and Khilafat wrongs.

Dec
Nagpur Congress Session adopts his resolution declaring object of Congress to be attainment of Swaraj by legitimate and peaceful means.

1921

30 Mar
In Vijayanagaram, pleads for Hindi to be made Lingua Franca of India.

Apr
Launches programme to set up twenty lakh charkhas in the country.

31 July
Leads Campaign for boycott of foreign cloth. Presides over huge bonfire at Bombay.

31 Oct
Takes vow of daily spinning.

19 Nov
Fasts for five days as protest against the communal riots.

Dec
Mass Satyagraha campaign begins, invested with full powers by Congress. Many Congress leaders arrested.

1922

4 Feb

Riots at Chauri Chaura.

12 Feb

Commences five day fast as protest against violence. Abandons plan of Satyagraha movement.

10 Mar

Arrested for sedition at Sabarmati. Sentenced to six years' imprisonment.

1924

4 Feb

Ordered release from prison.

17 Sept

Begins twenty-one day fast on behalf of Hindu Muslim Unity. Ends fast on 8 Oct.

1925

15 Feb

Inaugurates a national school and a Jain hostel at Rajkot.

22 Sept

Founds All India Spinners Association.

7 Nov

Madeleine Slade (Mirabehn) joins the Sabarmati Ashram.

29 Nov

Begins writing *The Story of My Experiments With Truth*.

1927

Jan – Nov

Extensive Khadi tour through North and South India.

1928

Dec

Moves resolution at Calcutta Congress in favour of Independence if Dominion Status is not granted by the end of 1929.

1929

3 Feb

Completes *The Story of My Experiments With Truth*.

4 Mar

Arrested for burning foreign cloth. Released later on personal recognition.

20 Aug
Declines Congress Presidentship. Suggests
  Pt. Jawaharlal Nehru instead.
27 Dec
Declares for complete Indian Independence
  at Lahore Congress.

1930
26 Jan
Declaration of Independence prepared
  by him is proclaimed all over India.
12 Mar
Begins Salt March from Sabarmati
  to Dandi.
6 Apr
Breaks salt jaw on the beach at Dandi. Launches
  Satyagraha throughout India.
18 Apr
Riots at Chittagong.
5 May
Arrested at Karadi and imprisoned at
  Yeravda gaol without trial. Hartal all over
  India. Over 100,000 are jailed before
  close of the year.

1931
26 Jan
Released together with other Congress
leaders.
4 Mar
Gandhi Irwin Pact signed.
12 Sept
Arrives in London to attend Round Table
  Conference, to meet with British leaders
  and elucidate the need for India's complete
  independence.
14 Dec
Sails to India after visiting Romain Rolland in
  Switzerland.

1932
4 Jan
Arrested in Bombay after his draft resolution
  for resumption of satyagraha is adopted by the
  Congress Working Committee. Detained at
  Yeravda gaol.
20 Sept
Begins fast unto death as protest against
  separate electorates for untouchables.

24 Sept
Yeravda Pact signed by high and low caste
  Hindus in the presence of Gandhi.
26 Sept
Concludes fast.

1933
Feb
While in prison, founds the Harijan Sevak
  Sangh and *Harijan*.

1933 – 34
Nov – June
Extensive tour on behalf of Harijans in north
  and south India, the last month of which is
  taken on foot.
17 Sept
Announces decision to retire from politics
  from 1st October to engage in development
  of village industries, Harijan Service and
  education through basic crafts.
24 Oct
Inaugurates all India Village Industries
  Association.

30 Oct
Resigns from Congress.

1940
Oct
Attends frequent Congress Working
  Committee meetings where he plays
  an active role. Suspends *Harijan* and
  allied weeklies following official demand
  for pre censorship on the subject of
  Satyagraha.
17 Oct
Launches limited civil disobedience
  campaign in protest against India's enforced
  participation in World War 2.

1942
18 Jan
Revives *Harijan* and allied weekly journals.
8 Aug
Launches Quit India movement.
9 Aug
Arrested and taken to Aga Khan's palace,
  Poona.

1944
22 Feb
Death of Kasturbai Gandhi while in prison at
  Poona.
9 Sept
Begins talks with Jinnah.
27 Sept
Announces breakdown of talks with Jinnah.

1945
17 Mar
Declares Vinoba Bhave and Kishorelal Mashruwala
  as his successors in Sevagram Ashram.

1946
Jan – Feb
Tours South India for anti untouchability and
  the learning of Hindustani.
Apr
Participates in political talks with Cabinet
  Mission in Delhi.
23 June
Advises Congress not to enter interim
  government proposed by Viceroy.

24 June
Meets Cabinet Mission.
7 July
Addresses Congress meeting in Bombay.
16 Aug
Four days rioting starts in Calcutta as the
  consequence of Direct Action called by the
  'Muslim League'.
27 Aug
Cables warning to British Government
  against repetition of 'Bengal Tragedy'.
 15 Oct
Muslim league enters Interim
  Government.

1947
2 Jan
Says 'All around me is utter darkness'.
3 – 29 Jan
Leaves Srirampur on walking tour. Tours riot
  affected areas in Bihar.
29 Mar
Lord Mountbatten, last Viceroy of India,
  arrives in India.

1–2 Apr
Addresses Asian Relations Conference in Delhi.
15 Apr
With Jinnah, issues joint appeal for communal
  peace.
5 May
Denies that communal division of India is
  inevitable.
2 June
Viceroy's Partition plan revealed and accepted.
6 June
Writes to Mountbatten to persuade Jinnah to settle
  amicably all outstanding points with Congress.
12 June
Addresses Congress Working Committee.
15 Aug
British India divided into two self-governing
  dominions; Gandhi rejoices for the deliverance
  from Brtish rule while deploring India's
  partition. Mass migration of Hindus and
  Muslims accompanied by widespread violence.
1 Sept
In Calcutta begins fast unto death. Fast broken
  after local peace is restored four days later.

1948
13 Jan
Begins fast in New Delhi on behalf of the
  communal unity.
17 Jan
Central Peace Committee formed and decides
  on 'Peace Pledge'.
18 Jan
Ends fast.
20 Jan
Bomb explosion at Birla House.
30 Jan
Struck by an assasin's bullet while on his way to
  evening prayer meeting. With hands folded in
  prayer and a gesture of forgiveness, he passed
  from this life with the words 'Hey Ram, Hey
  Ram' on his lips.

Bibliography

WORKS BY GANDHI

Hind Swaraj, or Indian Home Rule, 1938,
  Navajivan: Ahmedabad
*An Autobiography, or the Story of my
  Experiments with Truth*, 1927, Navajivan:
  Ahmedabad
Young India 1919-1922, 2nd ed., 1923, Ganesan:
  Chennai, Viking: New York
Young India 1924-1926, 1927, Ganesan:
  Chennai, Viking: New York
Young India 1927-1928, 1935, Ganesan:
  Chennai
From Yervada Prison, trans by Valji G. Desai,
  1947, Navajivan: Ahmedabad
For Pacifists, 1949, Navajivan: Ahmedabad
Satyagraha in South Africa, 1928, Ganesan:
  Chennai
*The Gospel of Selfless Action, or the Gita according
  to Gandhi*, 1946, Navajivan: Ahmedabad
Delhi Diary, 1948, Navajivan: Ahmedabad
Women and Social Injustice, 1942, Navajivan:
  Ahmedabad

COLLECTIONS OF GANDHI'S WRITINGS

India of my Dreams ed. by R.K. Prabhu, 1947,
  Hind Kitab: Mumbai
Selections from Gandhi ed. by Nirmal K. Bose,
  1948, Navajivan: Ahmedabad
My Early Life (1869-1914), 1947, ed. by
  Mahadev Desai, Oxford: London
To Students, 1935, Navajivan: Ahmedabad
Gleanings Gathered at Bapu's Feet ed. by
  Mira, 1929, 2nd ed., Navajivan: Ahmedabad
The Nation's Voice eds. by C. Rajagopalachari and
  J.C. Kumarappa, 1947, 2nd ed., Navajivan:
  Ahmedabad
Gandhi: His Life and Thought by J.B. Kripalani,
  1971, Publications Division, Ministry
  of Information and Broadcasting:
  New Delhi
Gandhi in India: In his own Words edited by Martin
  Green, 1987, Published for Tufts University
  by University Press of New England:
  Hanover, London
*Mahatma Gandhi's Ideas: Including Selections from
  his Writings* by C.F. Andrews, 1929, George
  Allen and Unwin: London
A Gandhi Anthology compiled by Valji Govindji
  Desai, 1952, Navjivan: Ahmedabad
Mahatma Gandhi at Work: His own story continued
  edited by C.F. Andrews, 1931, Allen and
  Unwin: London

Mahatma Gandhi: Selected Political Writings edited with an introduction, by Dennis Dalton, 1996, Hackett: Indianapolis

WRITINGS ABOUT GANDHI
The Life of Mahatma Gandhi by Louis Fischer, 1950, Harper: New York

Lead, Kindly Light by Vincent Sheean, 1949, Random House: New York

Gandhi's Leadership: The Oceanic Circle beyond Time and Geography by Jana Anand, 1999, Bharatiya Vidya Bhavan: Mumbai

Gandhi's Religious Thought by Margaret Chatterjee; Foreword by John Hick, 1983, University of Notre Dame Press: Notre Dame

Gandhi's View of Political Power by Jai Narain, 1987, Deep and Deep Publications: New Delhi

Gandhiji, the Ever Smiling Mahatma: An Anthology of Gandhian Humour by S. Durai Raja Singam, 1957, Kuantan: Malaya

Gandhiji Through my Diary Leaves 1915-1948 by Kanji Dwarkadas, 1950, Mumbai: the author

Gandhi as I know him by Indulal Kanaiyalal Yajnik, 1943, Danish Mahal: New Delhi

Gandhi: Father of a Nation by Catherine Clément, 1996, Thames and Hudson: London

Gandhi: The Forgotten Mahatma by Jagdishchandra Jain, 1987, Mittal Publications: New Delhi

All Men are Brothers: Life and Thoughts of Mahatma Gandhi as told in his own words. UNESCO [1958]

The Moral and Political Thought of Mahatma Gandhi by Raghavan N. Iyer, 1973, Oxford University Press: New York

The Life and Death of Mahatma Gandhi by Robert Payne, 1969, Bodley Head: London

Mahatma Gandhi: The Great Soul by Emil Lengyel, 1966, F. Watts: New York

Mahatma Gandhi: Essays and Reflections on his Life and Work, presented to him on his seventieth birthday, October 2nd, 1939. Together with a new memorial section, by Sarvepalli Radhakrishnan, Allen & Unwin: London

Mahatma Gandhi: the man who became one with the universal being by Romain Rolland, translated by Catherine D. Groth, 1924, The Century Co: New York, London

Mahatma Gandhi by Jawaharlal Nehru, 1966, Asia Publishing House: Bombay

In the footsteps of Mahatma Gandhi by Homer A Jack, 1952, S.N.: S.L.

Gandhi and the Status of Women by S.R. Bakshi, 1987, Criterion Publications: New Delhi

Index